VINTAGE

ALABAMA
SIGNS

Perhaps churches are not the first things most people think of when it comes to vintage signs, but especially in urban areas, neon crosses could be found in a wide variety of colors. Running a close second would be signs of this type, overhanging the sidewalk. *Dixie Neon collection.*

VINTAGE

ALABAMA SIGNS

TIM HOLLIS

THE
History
PRESS

Published by The History Press
Charleston, SC
www.historypress.com

Front cover, clockwise from top left: Dixie Neon collection; author's collection; author's collection; Dixie Neon collection; Russell Wells collection; author's collection.
Back cover: author's collection.

Unless otherwise noted, all images are courtesy of the author.

First published 2024

Manufactured in the United States

ISBN 9781467156110

Library of Congress Control Number: 2023946776

Notice: The information in this book is true and complete to the best of our knowledge. It is offered without guarantee on the part of the author or The History Press. The author and The History Press disclaim all liability in connection with the use of this book.

There was a time when the brand of trading stamps was one of the most important features in deciding whether to patronize a business. S&H Green Stamps were the leader, and in the early 1990s, this rusting advertisement still hung in a vacant lot that was once a gas station on US Highway 78.

Birmingham's Third Avenue North was justly famed as the centerpiece of the city's theater and retail district. Of all the establishments with their signs aglow in this 1965 view, only the Alabama Theatre remains, and its sign and marquee have recently been renovated to duplicate the appearance of their 1927 originals.

CONTENTS

The lonely Maytag Repairman of TV commercial fame might not have been needed to keep them running, but these coin laundries were seemingly everywhere at one time. Those commercial-grade Maytag washers must have been just about as dependable as the ads claimed.

ACKNOWLEDGEMENTS

Although most of the material you will see in the pages that follow originated in my own decades-long collection of memorabilia, kudos must be given to the additional sources that enlivened the result. As you will notice in the credit lines for the photos, a number of them (as well as other helpful information) came from fellow tourism collectors, historians and photographers: Rodney Barstein, Al Coleman, Wes Daniel, Steve Gilmer, Jim Hatcher, Jeannie Kuhlman, the late Ernest Langner of Dixie Neon, Christy Malone of Jack's Family Restaurants, Debra Jane Seltzer (www. roadarch.com), Delene Sholes of Ace Neon and Russell Wells.

We must also acknowledge the late photographer John Margolies, who bequeathed his personal archive to the Library of Congress with the amazing stipulation that no restrictions were to be imposed on its use by other authors and researchers.

The center court at Birmingham's Western Hills Mall must have been a great location for shoe stores, with Florsheim and Hardy Shoes staring each other down from respective corners. But what's going on in front of them, you ask? That is your faithful author in his days as a puppeteer, making his initial appearance with Alabama TV legend Cousin Cliff Holman in May 1982.

INTRODUCTION

Before we dive into this collection of photos of vintage Alabama signage, it might be a good idea to put it into some context. In many ways it should be considered the next volume in a series that includes the previous books *Birmingham's Theater and Retail District* (2005), *Vintage Birmingham Signs* (2008), *See Alabama First: The Story of Alabama Tourism* (2013) and *Lost Attractions of Alabama* (2019). In fact, in assembling this latest work, we had something of a challenge to not duplicate images that had already appeared in the others. We think we have done a pretty good job; if by chance you catch a photo that you have seen before, in all likelihood it is at least appearing here for the first time in color.

There is something else about this book that sets it apart from the others. Because so many of the images contained herein are ones that have some personal connection to me, you may find that I occasionally had to lapse into my own memories in order to describe them. (The Western Hills Mall photos that accompany this introduction are a good example.) I hope that will not be a deterrent to your own enjoyment and interpretation of the pictures, but unless I ever try to write an autobiography, this book may have more of my own life in it than any of the others.

Whether from my own archives or from other credited sources, these photos are rich in pop culture detail. In a limited amount of space allotted for captions, there is no way to adequately describe or point out every single item of interest in the images, so my advice is that you get out your trusty magnifying glass and go over them with an eagle eye, just to keep from missing things that might be lurking in the background or on the periphery that aren't necessarily mentioned in the text.

Although we do cover the entire state of Alabama, it must be admitted that the northern half probably does overbalance the southern half here. Part of that is due to simple population distribution, but also because one of the largest sign companies in Alabama, Dixie Neon, was based in Birmingham, and its unbelievable archives maintained by the late Ernest Langner provided much material for this and the preceding books mentioned earlier. Mr. Langner lived to be nearly one hundred years old and had an encyclopedic knowledge of every project his company had undertaken. I have not been in contact with any of his children since he passed away, but I hope they realize what a priceless trove of history they inherited from their dad.

As I have mentioned in other books, until seeing photos such as these, many people have never stopped to think about the important role signs have played in their memories. We are exposed to them practically from our first automobile ride when our parents brought us home from the maternity ward. My own folks told me that one of their first hints that I could read was when, at a young age, I started telling them what the billboards along the highway said. (Considering that I was nearsighted enough to need glasses by the time I was eight years old, there must have been some awfully huge lettering on those signs.) Many times as we travel through the following pages, you may surprise yourself by saying, "I remember that sign but I haven't thought about it in years!" Well, now's the time to start thinking about it again, pal, so turn the page and start thinking—and remembering.

ONE

SO MANY STORES IN
SO FEW PAGES

In the first chapter, we'll be looking at signs representing the various aspects of shopping. Many of them can be found in this typical street scene in Anniston. Drugstores, five-and-dime stores, shoe stores, restaurants and others are represented, and we will get a closer look at all of those types in the coming pages. *Steve Gilmer collection.*

TOP: For contrast, here is a 1976 view of the downtown Birmingham skyline, which is just about the opposite of the Anniston street scene. While many of these buildings still exist, the signage visible here does not: the Pizitz department store, the scrolling rooftop sign of the Bank for Savings building, the now-demolished Parliament House hotel, Central Bank and the Top of 21 nightclub.

OPPOSITE, BOTTOM: While we're on the subject of department stores, we might as well mention that Loveman's was one of the oldest in Birmingham. Its full name was Loveman, Joseph and Loeb, but by the time this signage was installed in the 1950s, popular usage had shortened it to just one cofounder's name.

LEFT: After Loveman's closed forever in the spring of 1980, this fading painted sign remained on the crosswalk that connected the store with its parking deck. Apparently, the bottom portion with the store hours had been repainted more recently than the upper portion listing the locations.

As almost everyone knows, Loveman's chief rival was the Pizitz chain. Its downtown store was a landmark, but this photo dates from the 1960s, when the chain had expanded into the suburbs—in this case, the Five Points West shopping complex. Somehow, one gets the impression those "shoppers" were just as posed as the mannequins in the display windows.

There was a brief period in the 1960s and early 1970s when the JCPenney chain decided to go modern and referred to itself simply as "Penney's." The photo dates from 1967, but the location of this Alabama shopping center was not documented. The blue "humpbacked" Penney's logo could be found at practically all the branches of that era. *Dixie Neon collection.*

It was not so long ago that no other retailer was as large as Sears, Roebuck and Co. Walking through those doors underneath that glowing green neon logo was like stepping inside Sears' annual Christmas Wish Book.

TOP: Now let's leave the department stores and visit the extreme opposite end of the retail spectrum, the neighborhood general store. This one near Oakman was photographed in 1983, when it still bore its signage advertising various brands of soft drinks. Its days as a functioning store, unfortunately, had long since fizzled out.

BOTTOM: In Mooresville, the old Bedingfield General Merchandise building has enjoyed several lives. Its slogan, "We doze, but never close," finally became untrue when the store went out of business in the 1990s, but as the structure has been used for other purposes, from a restaurant to a bicycle store, this former neon sign has been preserved as part of them all.

When several different types of stores began congregating around a shared parking lot, the concept of a "shopping center" was born. Birmingham's Five Points West Shopping City began taking shape shortly before World War II and eventually sprawled across both sides of US 11. This is one of the aforementioned examples in which close scrutiny will produce numerous delightful surprises. *Dixie Neon collection*.

OPPOSITE, TOP: The shopping center concept showed up in Huntsville in the form of Parkway City in 1957. This 1959 view shows the complex's appropriately rocket-themed signage as well as just some of the component stores. Parkway City was heavily damaged by a tornado in 1974. *Steve Gilmer collection.*

OPPOSITE, BOTTOM: By the time of this photo, the 1960s splendor of the Cullman Shopping Center sign on US 31 was beginning to fade. It was still easy to see that the starburst and flashing arrows would have been an eye-catching nighttime sight in their prime.

ABOVE: Roebuck Shopping Center was at the opposite end of US 11 in Birmingham from Five Points West. Look very closely between the poles of the sign, and you will spy with your little eye what may be the only color documentation of signage for the locally based Burger in a Hurry chain (about which more in the restaurants chapter). *Dixie Neon collection.*

After shopping centers, the next logical step was to add a roof and create a mall that was impervious to weather conditions. Eastwood Mall was the first such complex in Alabama when it opened in 1960. In this postcard view of the interior, note the teal-colored signage for the J.J. Newberry store on the right and a colorful logo for an RCA Victor record shop on the left.

OPPOSITE: In Anniston, Quintard Mall was named for its location on—what else?— Quintard Avenue, aka US 431. The second photo could have been included in our chapter on entertainment, as it shows the touring van of Cousin Cliff Holman and his early 1970s sponsor McDonald's. But it appears here because of the orange neon sign for the Britts department store chain. Little remembered today, it was part of the same company as J.J. Newberry.

F. W. Woolworth Co. Store, Birmingham, Ala.

Greetings From PHENIX CITY, ALABAMA

OPPOSITE, TOP: Don't you just love it when a single photo can encapsulate an entire era in pop culture? This clothing store inside Eastwood Mall practically screams "1975" with its bell-bottom trousers and simulated wood grain on the sign, not to mention the far-out, groovy posters in the windows, man. *Ace Neon collection*.

OPPOSITE, MIDDLE: When F.W. Woolworth pioneered the concept of a five-and-ten-cent store, he also began a tradition of such stores having names consisting of the founder's initials and last name. We have already seen G.C. Murphy at Parkway City and J.J. Newberry at Eastwood Mall, but others would include S.H. Kress, H.L. Green and a few more we shall see shortly. Each one developed its own trademark color scheme; the Woolworth stores used red and gold signage to stand out along any Main Street.

OPPOSITE, BOTTOM: Another store using the "initials" format for a name was W.T. Grant, with an orange-and-blue color palette. This one in downtown Birmingham had been converted into other businesses for decades, but a planned 2005 renovation uncovered remnants of the 1930s Grant's signage on the storefront.

ABOVE: At this Phenix City shopping center, rivals Woolworth's and Grant's stood cheek by jowl with Grant's giving S&H Green Stamps. Elsewhere in the same complex, a Big Apple supermarket was promoting one of the many competitors in the trading stamp wars, King Korn Stamps. *Steve Gilmer collection*.

ABOVE: An Alabama-based five-and-ten chain was V.J. Elmore, founded in Clanton. In fact, this is a Clanton location in that popular chain, although obviously not the original one. Note the diagonally split "5/10" logo on the aquamarine storefront, a pricing structure that was becoming increasingly rare when this 1964 photo was taken. *Barstein family collection.*

OPPOSITE, TOP & MIDDLE: By the 1980s, the Elmore stores had packed up their boxes and left town, leaving only sad remnants to show they had ever existed. The tile floor and door handle could still be seen at a vacant storefront in Greensboro as late as 2012.

OPPOSITE, BOTTOM: Long before Dollar General, there was Bargain Town USA, an Alabama chain with a remarkably similar marketing scheme. As seen in this 1960s photo, signage practically overwhelmed the merchandise. Featured on it all was the Bargain Town mascot, an unnamed flat-topped, bucktoothed character seen only as a face and occasionally a pointing hand. *Barstein family collection.*

OPPOSITE, TOP: By 1968, when this Bargain Town USA was photographed in Opelika, the logo character had gained a body and a name: Buckworth, the winning entry in a "Name the Bargain Town Man" contest. *Barstein family collection.*

OPPOSITE, BOTTOM: In time for the nation's bicentennial in 1976, Buckworth was given a facelift, gaining a full head of blond hair and a snazzy Uncle Sam suit. The location of this 1981 grand opening was not documented, but "Uncle Buckworth" was certainly in evidence everywhere (alongside a bunch of Bugs Bunny balloons). *Barstein family collection.*

ABOVE: Here's a transition you might have missed if you weren't playing attention. S.S. Kresge was originally another of the "initials" style of five-and-ten stores, but in 1962, it morphed into one of the first of what would become known as the "big box" discount stores, Kmart. Of course, we know that Kmart and Sears later merged, and now there are practically none of either store left for us to enjoy. *Dixie Neon collection.*

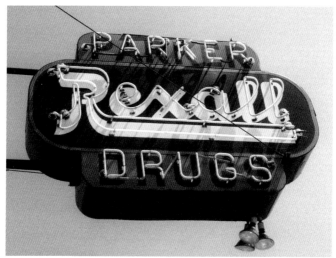

OPPOSITE, TOP: Another of the big discount store chains was Zayre. It was probably most popular in the 1970s and early 1980s, with locations in a number of Alabama cities. The chain went defunct in 1990, and more often than not, the huge empty buildings were carved up into numerous smaller businesses. *Ace Neon collection.*

OPPOSITE, MIDDLE: Now, let's talk about another major category of retail: drugstores. In the late 1940s and the 1950s, the biggest drugstore chain of them all was Rexall, and its orange-and-blue neon signs lit up many streets in both large and small towns. By 1991, this one on US 78 in Leeds was a rare survivor; even though the store is now closed and empty, this sign has been lovingly preserved to await its next life.

OPPOSITE, BOTTOM: Chain drugstores are now the dominant strain, but there have been thousands of small, independent pharmacies that put their own unique stamps on the industry. In 1984, this one in Adamsville decorated its building with signage featuring a character named Thrifty Mack Campbell—designed and voiced (in commercials) by the author of this book. Was there *nothing* he wouldn't do to stay in the public eye?

ABOVE: The traditional symbol of a pharmacy was the mortar and pestle (or did you not know what that object was called?). As we are about to see, it could take many different forms. Signs similar to this one, with a clock embedded in the mortar, could be found in a number of locations. *Dixie Neon collection.*

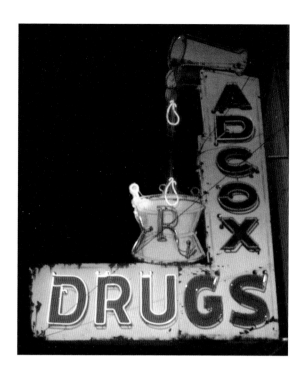

ABOVE: In contrast to the preservation of the Rexall sign a few pages back, this one in downtown Jasper met an awful fate. Only a few days after this nighttime shot, when the formerly animated neon pestle and dripping medicine were already frozen in place, the old veteran sign was removed from the building and hauled off to the scrapyard.

OPPOSITE, TOP: This colorful rendition is another one that no longer exists, although it had undergone a renovation just before this March 1991 photo. It was removed not in the name of modernization, but because the store went out of business and there was no further need for it.

OPPOSITE, MIDDLE: This store in Graysville is also long gone, but while it lasted, its three-dimensional rendition of the mortar and pestle was somewhat unusual. As with many independent pharmacies, the retirement or death of the owner spelled the end for the business as well. Today, only the metal skeleton of the symbol still stands atop the tower.

OPPOSITE, BOTTOM: A very successful Alabama pharmacy chain was Big B Discount Drugs, an offshoot of the mammoth Bruno's supermarket chain (about which more in our next chapter). From the late 1960s into the early 1980s, the Big B stores featured this yellow mortar and blue pestle, sometimes illuminated and sometimes not. Big B was later absorbed by the CVS chain. *Dixie Neon collection.*

OPPOSITE, TOP: Now, let's visit a few other miscellaneous types of retail stores. This pink-and-green neon masterpiece has been helping sell flowers on US 31 in Decatur since 1957 and in recent years has been refurbished to make sure its giant carnation will continue to bloom for years to come.

OPPOSITE, BOTTOM: Even though the once-popular Western Auto chain of stores was officially defunct by 2003, a few of its former locations stubbornly clung to their signage. This one in the Anniston/Oxford area was still holding on in March 2008.

ABOVE: Shoe stores sometimes had to sell their soles in order to make themselves stand out from their surroundings. This 1950s view of one in downtown Birmingham certainly shows the lengths to which owner Izz Eubanks would go in order to sell his shoes to walk-in customers, even to the point of plastering his face on the front of the building. *Dixie Neon collection.*

TOP: Another type of footwear was the cowboy boot, invariably promoted by stores with a Western theme. The Bootlegger, on US 31 at Fultondale, augmented its building with a giant boot that was sometimes adorned with Christmas lights for the holiday season. Where the store and boot once camped out is now nothing but a patch of kudzu and trees.

BOTTOM: Similar to Western Auto, Busch Jewelers had franchise stores in many states, with a localized name incorporated into the signage. This jewel of a neon sign for Happiness Jewelers could still be seen turning into rust (or back into coal, perhaps) in Talladega in the early 1990s.

In downtown Birmingham, across the street from the Alabama Theatre, jewelry/furniture store Lichter's was famous for its "Magic Credit" logo of a rabbit pulling a magician out of a hat. While the building was being renovated for use as apartments, this animated rendition of the logo (with the magician figure missing) was discovered in storage. Plans were to restore it for display purposes, but its current whereabouts are unknown.

ABOVE: As you might be able to tell from the angle of this photo, Mr. King Furniture was next door to Lichter's. It was earlier known as King Kredit, using the balding, snaggle-toothed monarch not only as its sign, as seen here, but also as an animated figure that sat in the store's entryway.

OPPOSITE, TOP: Not to be confused with today's Liberty Mutual insurance company of incessant TV commercials fame, Liberty National was based in Birmingham for more than eighty years. Its headquarters originally featured a neon sign representing the Statue of Liberty, but in 1965 it installed a giant bronze replica of the statue atop a rooftop pedestal. The statue was removed in 1989 but still exists as the emblem of an office complex on I-459 known, naturally, as Liberty Park. *Dixie Neon collection*.

OPPOSITE, BOTTOM: In its day, Liberty National was one of the most aggressive advertisers in Alabama, with more giveaway doodads than one could shake a torch at. Its metal signs could be found along major highways and back roads alike, and it curried favor with parents by erecting these shelters for schoolkids awaiting their buses.

ABOVE: Let's face it, most of the signs of the type documented in this book no longer exist, but sometimes the lucky ones turn up in antiques stores. This store in Sheffield had an impressive collection of them, but it closed during the 2020 COVID-19 pandemic. Reportedly, its contents are safely warehoused somewhere.

OPPOSITE, TOP: It can be interesting when even a former antiques store can become an antique. This one, in a converted service station, stood at an I-59 exit near Valley Head, with no evidence of either of its former lives except a fading sign.

OPPOSITE, MIDDLE: In 2013, this enormous White House Antique Mall complex on US 431 north of Guntersville, a former nursing home, appeared to have been abandoned for quite some time. But its appearance might have been deceiving, as a peek into the windows showed some dealers' merchandise still inside, apparently left to the elements after the store closed.

OPPOSITE, BOTTOM: One of the earliest stores in Alabama to use the term *antique mall* was this one on US 31 in Gardendale. With several newer stores of its type in the area, it finally threw in its collectibles and closed in the spring of 2023. This faded sign could be interpreted as a representation of its faded glory.

One category of sign we have barely mentioned so far belonged to appliance stores. Although both of these examples are plastic rather than neon or metal, they still represent a bygone era, and both were part of the US 78 roadside. The Whirlpool sign stood in Heflin, while the Zenith sign was in Carbon Hill, a stretch of 78 that became desolate after the long-awaited I-22 siphoned away the traffic heading to and from Memphis.

TWO

CHECKING OUT YOUR GROCERY LIST

Now we shall visit a subset of the whole shopping experience, namely grocery stores and advertising for the products they sold. And, in a subset of a subset, we begin with the tradition of "vanity signs." This is an example of one. It has stood over a closed building in Dora for decades. Vanity signs had a company logo with the added personalization of the owner's name. That part of the neon had crumbled into illegibility long before this photo was taken.

ABOVE: On the former US 78 (the old Bankhead Highway) just east of Sumiton, the grocery store run by Clayton "Doc" Sellers had this vanity sign furnished by Coca-Cola. The store building is long gone, and so is the sign, but the pole that supported it could still be seen as of this writing.

OPPOSITE, TOP: How many people familiar with RC Cola remember that the initials stand for Royal Crown? Even though this was a service station near Jasper and not a grocery store, it still managed to finagle its own vanity sign from the soda-pop producer. All traces of this business have disappeared since this 1983 photo was taken.

OPPOSITE, MIDDLE: Barber's Dairy was responsible for many vanity signs across Alabama, and this one on the former Paul Marsh and Son general store in Locust Fork has become something of a shrine for fans of advertising history. These cheerful red-and-yellow creations always seemed to make customers feel welcome. *Russell Wells collection.*

OPPOSITE, BOTTOM: This lighted Barber's sign must have been a glorious sight in its day. The magenta-and-white Barber's Milk wax cartons remained virtually unchanged for decades until the company was purchased by out-of-state interests in 1997. Modernizing the packaging might or might not have had anything to do with Barber's final closure in 2021.

Another once-ubiquitous Alabama dairy brand was Deep South, with plants in both Cullman and Jasper. Its red-and-green color motif could be seen on its cartons, promotional products and a metal sign that was still holding its ground near Blount Springs in the early 1990s. The fading painted wall sign was on the same closed grocery store that opened this chapter; it has long since been painted over.

Foremost was a national dairy brand and not simply local to Alabama, but its promotional items are now highly desirable collectibles. At some point around 1969 (information borders on the nonexistent), Foremost changed its name to Farmbest, with a weathervane logo. The Marsh Grocery sign in Warrior—not to be confused with the aforementioned Paul Marsh and Son—undoubtedly dated from that period.

ABOVE: In the realm of Alabama snack foods, few other trademarks were as familiar as Golden Flake's potato chips and the clown character that seemed to be modeled somewhat on Ringling Brothers star Lou Jacobs. Like Barber's Dairy, Golden Flake was eventually purchased by non-Alabama interests. The clown was sent back to his circus tent, but the brand name survives—at least for now.

OPPOSITE, TOP: Yellow Label Syrup was another Alabama institution. This giant replica of its packaging, pancakes dripping with butter, rotated atop the company plant in downtown Birmingham. That building is now gone, but we can all hope that this gargantuan jar may still exist in someone's garage or warehouse.

OPPOSITE, BOTTOM: Do you remember when Millbrook Bread was one of a number of bakeries nationwide that used the Charles Schulz *Peanuts* characters in its advertising? They were even painted as signage on the company's delivery trucks, and at one point this abandoned example, with Charlie Brown fading into the past, was spotted in a junkyard in Sumiton. Good grief!

OPPOSITE, TOP: For more than fifty years, the name *Bruno's* was synonymous with grocery stores in Alabama. In the late 1960s, the Bruno's signage had evolved into these hexagonal letters that adorned most of their newest locations. This fine example was in Irondale in 1967. *Dixie Neon collection.*

OPPOSITE, BOTTOM: The debonair Bruno Bear, with his dignified bow tie, appeared consistently in Bruno's newspaper ads, but he made far fewer appearances on their external signage. One exception was this store in Gardendale, which, as we can see, shared space with Bruno's pharmacy division, Big B Discount Drugs. *Dixie Neon collection.*

ABOVE: By the early 1980s, most of the traditional Bruno's stores were being phased out in favor of its "big box" equivalent, Food World. A 1991 plane crash tragically killed the top five Bruno's executives, and the company went into a downward spiral. By 2012, even the Food World brand was going out of this world.

ABOVE: On Birmingham's Finley Avenue, Richard's Meats beckoned to the public with this beautiful pink-and-blue neon butcher who moved his legs and cleaver at a dizzying pace. As with most such neon creations, he was put on the chopping block many years ago.

OPPOSITE: In the early 1900s, a tonic marketed under the name VegaCal erected these somewhat disconcerting iron figures at crossroads throughout northern Alabama, giving directions rather like the Scarecrow in *The Wizard of Oz*. This one in Hartselle is the sole known survivor, even supplying a name to an adjacent grocery store and Iron Man Road. *Russell Wells collection.*

In an ill-fated attempt to bring the idea of themed entertainment to the grocery store world, the interior of Gardendale's Robin Hood Super Store strove for the look of Sherwood Forest, with the employees forced to dress as Merrie Men. Apparently the public was not ready for Disney-type shenanigans while trying to purchase milk and eggs. *Dixie Neon Collection.*

Stores of many different types we have mentioned so far can be seen in this late 1960s/early 1970s view of the State Highway 79 strip in Center Point. Since we are about to delve into the tasty world of restaurants, feast your peepers on such long-gone institutions as the A-frame Der Weinerschnitzel, a Burger Chef and one of the area's legendary Spinning Wheel drive-ins. *Dixie Neon Collection.*

THREE

FOOD, BOTH FAST AND SLOW

We now turn our attention to notable restaurant signage, and few signs could have been as iconic as the animated spectacular at Goal Post Bar-B-Q in Anniston. The neon football player would repeatedly kick a pigskin through the uprights, which would then tumble and rotate onto the building's roof via sixteen neon stages. The sign continues to kick a few blocks from its original location, at Betty's Bar-B-Q.

ABOVE: A long-standing tradition in barbecue restaurant signage is a pig dressed as a chef, providing decidedly cannibalistic overtones. The sign for Big Bob Gibson Bar-B-Q on US 31 in Decatur is said to date back to 1952.

OPPOSITE, TOP: There were once some fourteen locations of Bob Sykes Bar-B-Q throughout Alabama, and most (if not all) of them employed some version of this sign's design. The happy hog on the yellow panel seems disturbingly delighted to be serving one of his relatives in a barbecue Porky sandwich.

ABOVE: Some restaurants and their signage just seem to fade into the forest. Such is the case of this one on US 231 (where else?), just north of Dothan. If not for its bright yellow background, it might be totally unnoticeable.

ABOVE: We now move from barbecue to hamburgers and arrive much, much farther north on US 231 in Arab. Local landmark Midas Burger now has a more modern sign than the one they were using in 1991, but behind the restaurant, the original can still be seen—in even rougher shape than it was here.

OPPOSITE: Big Chief Hamburgers in Glencoe occupies a distinctive building that was once part of a chain called Chip's Drive-Ins. Their A-frame structures with brightly colored panels make former Chip's locations easy to identify.

OPPOSITE, TOP: Alabama's most famous hamburger chain, dating back to 1960, is Jack's. It evolved from drive-ins into today's sit-down restaurants. The earliest Jack's locations had a loud yellow-and-orange-striped porcelain enamel finish and a distinctive five-post sign spelling out the name and other features. *Jack's Family Restaurants collection.*

OPPOSITE, BOTTOM: Over the years, modernization did its usual thing, and finally only one of the original five-post Jack's signs was still being used by the company. It was the one in Dora, and this photo was taken in December 2018 on the night before it was scheduled to be taken down. Jack's reports that it was placed in storage to await a decision on how best to use it in the future.

ABOVE: In the late 1960s, Jack's opened a small store on First Avenue North in downtown Birmingham. As the building was being demolished in 2015, removal of the facade revealed the original yellow-and-orange-striped enamel still lurking underneath.

ABOVE: Even after Jack's had phased out the five-post signs, some of them still stood in front of former locations and were repurposed to fit their new ownership. This one on the Bessemer Superhighway (US 11) had obviously switched its loyalty from hamburgers to hot dogs. *Dixie Neon collection.*

OPPOSITE: What's going on here? Yes, Fort Payne had a Jack's Hamburgers that predated the official chain, so it was allowed to continue using the name. The Fort Payne Jack's (which, incidentally, occupied yet another of the A-frame Chip's buildings) has since been converted into a Mexican restaurant, and only parts of this flashy structure can still be seen.

At about the same time Jack's was getting started, another chain came out of Birmingham: Burger in a Hurry. Its signs and buildings were coated in red-and-green neon, mostly in various-sized boomerang shapes. The company mascot, pointy-eared Mr. Realee Good, could be seen everywhere.

TOP: Frosty Inn had locations in many states, but at all of them the most identifiable trademark was the brown root beer barrel on the roof. This is the Frosty Inn of Russellville, which first opened in 1960 and is still a landmark in that town.

BOTTOM: Another drive-in chain with a barrel on the roof was Mug 'n' Cone. It had outlets throughout northern Alabama, and whereas Burger in a Hurry used boomerangs, Mug 'n' Cone went for diamond shapes in a big way. Get a load of the multicolored diamonds in this generic postcard promoting the company.

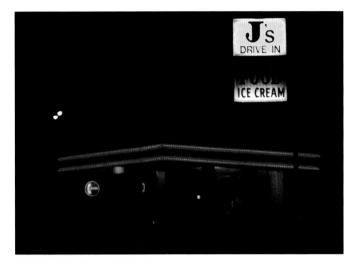

OPPOSITE, TOP: Some small-town drive-ins were disarmingly simple. Without fancy shapes or advertising characters, J's Drive-In on US 78 in Adamsville was satisfied to outline its roof with red neon. (Note another defunct type of signage in this nighttime view: the lighted sign for a pay telephone.) The building has now shifted to the other end of the nutritional scale and serves as a Subway sandwich shop.

OPPOSITE, BOTTOM: There seems to be no definite clue as to the location of this Dairy Frost drive-in, but its neon burger and shake must have been a welcome sight to drivers along that highway—wherever it might have been. *Ace Neon collection.*

ABOVE: There is no question as to where this abandoned and deteriorating Dairy Delite sits. The Clanton eatery and its neon chicken and curly ice cream cone have become a popular subject for roadside history photographers. There is still an operating Dairy Delite in Clanton, but it does not seem to get nearly as much attention as the defunct one.

In the 1960s and 1970s, it was quite common to see buildings using this green-and-yellow-striped corrugated plastic in many different forms. This was on the back side of a former drive-in in downtown Jasper, but like the rest of the building, it has since been replaced with more subdued siding.

The Big Bull Steakhouse at Cropwell was connected with the Brothers Four Motel. The animated neon bovine on the sign assured hungry herds of travelers that they wouldn't get a bum steer. *Debra Jane Seltzer collection.*

OPPOSITE: A different longhorn could be seen rotating inside the barn doors of the Bonanza Sirloin Pit signs. The chain, which was initially promoted by the cast members of its namesake TV series, had numerous locations in Alabama, and this sign could have been at any of them. *Wes Daniel collection.*

ABOVE: Not to be confused with the Bugtussle that was the hometown of the Beverly Hillbillies, this Bugtussle is on State Highway 69, about halfway between Jasper and Cullman. Its steakhouse drew drooling drivers from miles around, and years after it closed (and the original building burned down), like the Star-Spangled Banner, its sign was still there.

The Catfish King chain had several locations in Birmingham, including this one in Woodlawn (in a converted funeral home, yet), seen here in 1964. Common to all the Catfish Kings was the neon sign depicting a leaping blue catfish with a golden crown and the bright yellow starbursts detailing its many special dinners. *Dixie Neon collection*.

OPPOSITE: About the time Catfish King bit the hook, the very similar Catfish Cabin chain rose to the surface to take its place. It, too, featured a blue neon catfish on its signage. *John Margolies collection*.

OPPOSITE, TOP: Most of the outlets of Pasquale's Pizza used this logo as their signage, with the pink-and-white stripes and somewhat top-heavy mustachioed chef. We can probably assume his name was Pasquale, even though that was not made explicit.

OPPOSITE, BOTTOM: The Pizza Boy store on Quintard Avenue in Anniston used this logo character on its sign. Yes, you probably guessed that Pizza Boy was a thinly reworked version of the more famous Big Boy of double-decker hamburger fame.

ABOVE: Drivers on US 31 in Clanton can see this not-so-little Little Caesar of the eponymous "pizza, pizza" chain. Although not unique, there are far fewer of these statues along the roadways than there ever were of the checkered-overalled Big Boy.

OPPOSITE, TOP: The heyday of Chuck E. Cheese's Pizza Time Theater could probably be pinpointed as the early 1980s. This sign in Gadsden was still in place some ten years later, with the earliest version of Chuck E. himself, looking more like a carnival barker than today's more juvenile rat.

OPPOSITE, BOTTOM: In the 1920s, ethnic restaurants were quite a novelty. The Joy Young Chinese restaurant opened at this location in downtown Birmingham in 1925. Its colorful, theater-style neon marquee was still glowing brightly the night this photo was taken—Joy Young's last evening of business in September 1980. (The marquee attracted so much attention that many people probably missed seeing the additional painted brick wall sign.)

ABOVE: Way back in our first chapter, remember the sign for the now-closed Gardendale Antique Mall? Here is what was on that spot alongside US 31 before the antiques: the Grub Stake Restaurant and Dry Gulch Ghost Town, rustling up food amid an enviable collection of authentic Western relics. Unfortunately, it was all consumed by a fire in 1969, and the building that would become the antiques store was constructed on the same concrete slab floor.

Stand 'n' Snack was a Birmingham chain with an unusual twist. Instead of freestanding buildings, all the locations were inside office buildings or, sometimes, shopping malls. The name was appropriate, as there were no tables or chairs. In this view, note the sign in the background promoting another Birmingham culinary hotspot, Dale's Cellar. *Dixie Neon collection.*

In 1976, Birmingham's south side had a whole strip of upscale restaurants that were very popular with those who wanted a spot for a date in their leisure suit or bell-bottom pants. This ad helpfully listed all of them and illustrated at least some of their nighttime signage.

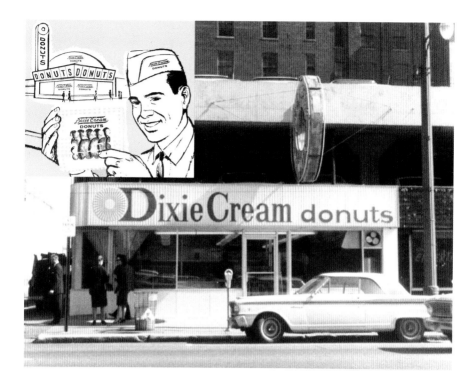

ABOVE: We'll be visiting Krispy Kreme soon, but before they were the doughnuts of choice for fundraising groups, that hole was filled by Dixie Cream Donuts. Their blue-and-white gingham boxes with a golden doughnut as part of the logo were sold by football teams, churches and cheerleaders alike. *Dixie Neon collection.*

OPPOSITE: Until it was killed by the COVID-19 pandemic, this "Donut Shoppe" in Muscle Shoals could make even a fiberglass doughnut look tempting with its chocolate-colored coating. Better put on your biggest choppers before biting into that delight.

ABOVE: Art's Char House replaced an older eatery known as the Dog House near the University of Alabama campus in Tuscaloosa. This 1962 photo shows that the sign fell firmly into the "Googie" style normally associated with Southern California, with its bouncing lettering against multicolored panels. *Dixie Neon collection.*

OPPOSITE: On US 11 just south of Attalla, this streamlined building seems to have gone under the names Eva's (on vintage postcards) and Wimp's (the signage left on the building). Under either name, its design indicates that it was part of the Standard Oil / Pan-Am chain of gas stations. But even though the property would initially seem to have been deserted for decades, a glance at the surviving menu board says otherwise. Those prices, and the Pepsi logo, are not too far in the past.

OPPOSITE, TOP: Now we turn our attention to chain restaurants, and one of the first chains in the USA was Howard Johnson's. Long before the name was a motel brand, Howard Johnson's spread its orange roofs and aqua spires "from Maine to Florida," as the advertising put it. Alabama had Howard Johnson's outlets statewide, from Florence to Mobile and from Tuscaloosa to Anniston. Its neon signs made celebrities out of Mother Goose veterans Simple Simon and the Pieman. *Dixie Neon collection*.

OPPOSITE, BOTTOM: From 1955 until approximately 1962, McDonald's used this neon masterpiece with its animated depiction of the hamburger-headed mascot Speedee. This one on Memorial Parkway in Huntsville was one of the only remaining examples by the 1990s. Fortunately, it was saved from demolition and fully restored, and Speedee now marches all day long at the American Sign Museum in Cincinnati.

ABOVE: If any company can be said to have used the "building as sign" concept, it would have been McDonald's. These red-and-white-striped edifices with glowing yellow arches stood out from their landscape, day or night. This one in Birmingham's Central Park neighborhood was widely believed to be the last example in Alabama when it was demolished in the late 1980s.

OPPOSITE, TOP: When the three original 1962 McDonald's stores in Birmingham were closed, pieces of their historical architecture were initially incorporated into the more modern buildings that replaced them. The McDonald's in Ensley saved the red-and-white tile and a portion of one of the illuminated arches. (That's the author's dad chowing down on a Filet-O-Fish sandwich in this 1984 photo.) None of the artifacts are known to have been preserved through subsequent remodeling.

OPPOSITE, BOTTOM: Kelly's Hamburgers was not an Alabama-based company, but it had a number of locations in the Birmingham and Tuscaloosa areas. The one in the center was originally an outpost of the Wagon Ho! chain, whose buildings were shaped like giant covered wagons with a Gabby Hayes lookalike driver on the buckboard.

ABOVE: Surely you remember the classic 1960s style of the Kentucky Fried Chicken sign, with its chasing lights and rotating illuminated bucket. One of them was still operating in Jasper in 1983.

OPPOSITE: When a KFC closed or moved, more often than not the bucket went with it. This location on US 431 in Anniston, however, became a Mexican restaurant and somehow managed to convert the Colonel's bucket into a Coca-Cola cup, complete with protruding straw. It has since been consigned to the trash heap.

ABOVE, TOP: On Mt. Meigs Road in Montgomery, this former KFC bucket did not even have the good fortune of a makeover. Photographed on a rainy day in November 2022, the gloomy weather only seemed to add a melancholy veneer to this sad sight.

ABOVE, BOTTOM: Earlier, we said we would visit a Krispy Kreme, and sure enough, this 1980s panoramic view shows not only that company's outlet at Eastwood Mall but also several other nearby now-defunct businesses' signage. (Can you spot the Parisian department store, Zayre and SouthTrust Bank?) At far right, note the sign for Grandy's Fried Chicken. It still exists as a chain but has no locations in Alabama.

The Jerry's chain of restaurants was once quite prominent in more northern states but managed to make only a few inroads into Alabama. This Jerry's (with the *J* in the logo shaped like a hot dog) spent its brief life at the junction of I-65 and US 278 in Cullman. A car dealership now occupies its former site. *Wes Daniel collection.*

FOUR

THAT'S A GAS

This chapter is primarily devoted to gas stations and other automobile-related
businesses. But before automobiles, people got around by railroads, and Birmingham's
old Union Station sat where the skyscraper in the background of this photo was built.
Replacing it was the 1960 L&N Station, with its distinctive mural showing the various
types of locomotives used by the Louisville and Nashville Railroad over the years. (Those
who were kids in the 1970s might remember the upper floor of the L&N structure
for its use as a walk-through attraction called Santa's Station for a few Christmases.)
The station—mural, Santa and all—was later demolished for Birmingham's current
intermodal facility.

OPPOSITE, TOP: An entire book could be filled with images of car dealerships, so for our purposes we will let this one stand in for all of them. And a most typical one it is, from the electric clock on its sign to the miles of multicolored plastic pennants fluttering in the breeze—actually, a form of signage themselves. *Dixie Neon collection.*

OPPOSITE, BOTTOM: Now we come to our first gas station signage. The "torch and oval" was familiar to several generations of motorists. At various times it represented Standard Oil, Pan-Am and the American Oil Company (aka Amoco). Even though "flat" signs such as this one were illuminated by floodlights, the flame of the torch would have its own internal lighting.

ABOVE: At the junction of US 29 and US 80 in Tuskegee, the shell of the Torch Café betrays its origins as a product of the Standard / Pan-Am / Amoco era. Note the similarity in design to the Wimp's building in the previous chapter and the torch on the building's front, now missing its lighted flame.

OPPOSITE, TOP: When this photo was taken on US 31 in Hoover, Standard was in its transition period to using the Chevron name for its brand. That dirt you see in the center background was the approaching I-65. Judging from the presence of the Holiday Inn sign, the nation's innkeeper already had the information that a major interchange was about to be constructed at that spot. *Dixie Neon collection.*

OPPOSITE, BOTTOM: Far away from any interstate routes or urban areas, this little store sat at the Jefferson/Walker County line on US 78. As you can see, Shell was its preferred brand of gas, and in the early 1990s, it still had one of the old red-and-yellow Shell signs with the dimensional seashell.

ABOVE: You could trust your car to the man who wore the star—the big, bright Texaco star—at this complex near Eastwood Mall in 1972. There's one of those 1960s-style KFC signs again, and the eye-catching striped pagoda building, but this time the rotating bucket seems to have spun away. *Dixie Neon collection.*

Another style of Texaco sign was this "tower," which could be seen from quite a distance, especially at night. (One can be spotted in the background of the previous photo.) This rusting example can still be found, as of this writing, on US 31 at Gardendale. Count the supports, kiddies, and you will be able to see where the giant T-E-X-A-C-O letters once glowed brightly.

The Sinclair gas stations used dinosaurs in their advertising dating back to the 1930s as a way of promoting the age of their crude oil. A series of statues of the prehistoric beasts was fabricated for the 1964–65 New York World's Fair and afterward went on tour throughout the country. In March 1967, they made a stop at Roebuck Plaza, so we not only get to see the Sinclair logo but also a row of the storefronts in that shopping center, all in living color. *Both, Jeannie Kuhlman collection.*

OPPOSITE: Look closely at the far end of this crowd scene and you will see the sign advertising Dino Souvenirs. Many kids still have their dinosaur doodads that were sold at this traveling exhibit, including paperback booklets and the hollow wax Mold-A-Rama figures that were made while you watched.

ABOVE: The Pure Oil sign was one of the most commonly seen at gas stations from the 1920s to the late 1960s. Although Pure made a comeback in the 1990s, this example in Copeland's Ferry was a relic of the company's original successful run.

In 1970–71, the former Pure stations began to be rebranded as Union 76. This ancient pump stood in front of the Paul Marsh and Son general store we saw in our groceries chapter. Look closely above the dollars window and you can still see the fading Pure logo from before the Union 76 days. *Russell Wells collection.*

Promoting the switch from Pure to Union 76 involved one of the most unusual ad campaigns in gas station history. Tying in with the "orange ball" Union 76 logo, stations gave out these packets of orange Funny Face drink mix imprinted with the new name. A nickel value!

OPPOSITE, TOP: Prior to the early 1970s, practically all gas was cheap, but there were some service station chains that were known for discounting the already-low prices. One such Alabama chain was SanAnn, with a pink-and-aqua color scheme on its buildings and boomerang shapes on its signage. In 1991, this SanAnn was still pumping in Owens Crossroads.

OPPOSITE, MIDDLE: The Wavaho stations are still with us, but you will not often see one with the characteristic giant signage of this one in Blountsville. Most of the "discount gas" stations advertised this way, with billboard-type signs that screamed at drivers to stop and fill up.

OPPOSITE, BOTTOM: This view of US 78 west of downtown Birmingham has almost too many gas station signs to mention, but in the distance please note the yellow-and-blue geometric wonder that represented the Site chain, one of the entrants in the "every surface a billboard" derby. Barely visible behind a telephone pole is the large sign for Miller's, another of the 1960s discount department stores of the Kmart, Woolco and Zayre variety.

ABOVE: This small station in Sumiton was once part of the Mutual chain, the brand with a running rabbit on its signage. By the time of this photo, the rabbit had hopped off down the bunny trail, but the building still had its three Coca-Cola "button" signs, outlined with neon that no longer worked.

ABOVE: Cougar Oil is still based in Selma, which is where John Margolies found this sign during one of his travels through Alabama. Remembering that the Lincoln-Mercury dealerships once used a live cougar as their emblem, putting Cougar gas into one of those must have produced an unstoppable road machine. *John Margolies collection.*

OPPOSITE: The Campbell 66 Express trucking company rolled out of Springfield, Missouri, but its fleet of trucks with the running image of panting Snortin' Norton the Camel could be seen on highways far and wide. This sign was at their local terminal on Birmingham's Finley Avenue. *Dixie Neon collection.*

While out driving, one was likely to encounter at least a few of these cautionary signs, especially near U.S. Forest Service outposts. As most folks have probably noticed, today the slogan has been modified from "forest fires" to "wildfires," since that term covers the broader problem. Smokey and his rangers still have to be on their guard.

FIVE

A ROOM FOR THE NIGHT

After all that eating and driving, we must all feel like checking into a good motel room for the night. There is a rather sad memory connected with this one. In March 1967, my parents and I set out for our first trip to Florida's Silver Springs. We made it from Walker County to Dothan before stopping at this motel for the evening, only to call family back home and learn that my great-grandfather had died that day. As a youngster, I couldn't understand why we had to turn around and go back home the next morning, but his funeral was held on my fourth birthday. (We finally made it to Silver Springs later that summer.)

While we are on the subject of driving to Florida, we might as well visit some of the other motels that millions of Alabamians saw on those trips. This one was south of Montgomery on US 231, the main route to the beaches of Florida's Miracle Strip. The motel is still in business but no longer under this name or with this landmark sign.

Farther down US 231 near Brundidge is this overgrown ruin, which has been a wreck for so long that even the name that was once on the sign has been obscured. The word *springs* seems to be part of the remaining neon, but that is all we can say about it.

OPPOSITE: Finally, Dothan had the Bee Line Motel on US 231, only a few miles north of the Florida state line. At one time it might have been a honey of a place to stay, but photographer Debra Jane Seltzer reports that as of 2020, only the vertical "motel" portion of the sign remained. *Debra Jane Seltzer collection.*

ABOVE: A few pages back, we mentioned the Holiday Inn that was built at the future junction of US 31 and I-65 in Hoover. This motel was another that moved into the neighborhood before the interstate came to town. Its fortunes have been up and down ever since, and it has gone through a dizzying number of brand names. Currently, the former Lamplighter Restaurant has been serving as Barrister's Tavern.

OPPOSITE, TOP: Birmingham's Tutwiler Hotel was the preferred place to stay for celebrities visiting the city; it was demolished in 1974. Do you wonder about that big blank space between "The" and "Tutwiler"? For decades, it was part of the Dinkler Hotels chain, and the sign read "The Dinkler Tutwiler." This late 1960s photo, taken during the annual Veterans Day parade, dates from after Dinkler was dunked.

OPPOSITE, BOTTOM: The Parliament House became Birmingham's hotel showplace after the Tutwiler's glory faded. Opened in early 1964, it brought the look and signage of a coastal Florida hotel to the city's south side. Its aqua-colored exterior and glowing yellow crown made it stand out from its surroundings. After years of decline, it was demolished in early 2008.

ABOVE: Before motels could be found at every interstate exit, even smaller towns needed their own hotels. Fort Payne had the Quin Hotel, which had 100 percent vacancy by the time of this early 1990s photo. Note the empty section with incandescent bulbs below the neon lettering for some now-unknown signage purpose.

OPPOSITE: Huntsville was already capitalizing on its role in the U.S. space program when the Dixie Neon company was contracted to produce this huge sign for the Space Capitol Motel. It appears the facility was not quite ready to blast off when this construction shot was taken. *Dixie Neon collection.*

ABOVE: Motel Birmingham was next door to the Howard Johnson's restaurant on US 78, near the future location of Eastwood Mall. At some point around 1960, it gained this classic "diving lady" sign, of the type many motels used to advertise their swimming pools. The former site is now a Veterans Administration facility. *Russell Wells collection.*

OPPOSITE: The Moon Winx Lodge with its winking neon crescent moon was a familiar sight to football fans driving into Tuscaloosa on University Boulevard. The lower portion of the sign had been modernized by the time the motel was condemned in early 2023. The sign was promptly removed and stored, awaiting its next life. *Debra Jane Seltzer collection.*

ABOVE: We have seen a number of advertising mascot characters so far—and will see more—but it was somewhat unusual for a local non-chain motel to have one. Doby's Hotel Court in Montgomery was an exception, featuring this neon southern colonel not only on its sign but also on most of its promotional items. *John Margolies collection.*

OPPOSITE, TOP: Research has failed to turn up just who Vann Thomas was or why his neon name was so prominent on this motel sign in Anniston. All we know is that, like so many of its contemporaries, the property eventually deteriorated into sleaze and had lost this sign long before the land was cleared in 2015.

OPPOSITE, BOTTOM: There was nothing distinctive about the architecture of Motel Samantha on US 78 in Oxford, but that sign was certainly bewitching. Its postcards advertised the presence of a Howard Johnson's restaurant next door, so that should have clinched the deal for anyone thinking of staying there.

ABOVE: Earlier photos of the Town Motel on Birmingham's western side show a tiny, nondescript sign. The Dixie Neon files dated this photo as September 1957, which must have been close to the time they constructed a larger and more elaborate sign. The influence of the Holiday Inn "Great Sign" is obvious. In the distance, you might be able to barely see Birmingham's 7Up bottling plant, with the logo atop a tall pylon. *Dixie Neon collection.*

At times, outlandish signage could turn up in the most unexpected places. The SuAnn Motel sign looked like it belonged at the beach but instead could be seen along US 231 in Arab. It, too, featured a starburst element but not closely resembling Holiday Inn's pulsating star.

Now, here's one with a more obvious copy of the Holiday Inn star. The Olsson Motel in Mobile has been around for some eighty years, but that starburst was added in the 1960s. According to photographer Debra Jane Seltzer, it had imploded into a black hole by 2021. *Debra Jane Seltzer collection.*

OPPOSITE, TOP: As US 11 wound through Collinsville on its way to Chattanooga, tired tourists might have been lured into stopping by this rather simple but appealing sign. The motel was out of business by 2002.

OPPOSITE, MIDDLE: Since we've yapped so much about signs that borrowed from the Holiday Inn "Great Sign," we might as well take another look at a genuine example. Coastal motels always had a look all their own, and the Holiday Inn in Gulf Shores was no exception, with its open-air balconies and palm tree landscaping.

OPPOSITE, BOTTOM: Earlier we mentioned how the Howard Johnson's Motor Lodges came to replace the company's earlier roadside restaurants. One change in the signage was that Simple Simon had previously been paired with the Pieman, but on the motel signage the kid had a new partner in the personage of an old lamplighter of long, long ago. This example was in Florence.

ABOVE: This September 2022 photo isn't vintage, but it shows the Howard Johnson's motel in Dothan. In recent years, a few (but by no means all) of the outlets in that chain have tried to recapture at least some of the original look, reinstating their orange roofs and aqua trim. No cupola, spire or Simple Simon has yet made a comeback, though.

ABOVE: The Alamo Plaza motel chain was, as should be obvious, based in Texas, but its Alabama locations operated under the name of St. Francis Hotel Courts. This location was in Mobile and followed the parent company's "building as sign" tradition by placing replicas of the Alamo on the fronts of otherwise nondescript buildings. *Al Coleman collection.*

OPPOSITE: Mascot characters did not catch on in the motel industry as much as they did with restaurants, with Holiday Inn's colonial innkeeper John Holiday, Ramada Inn's butler Uncle Ben and Howard Johnson's lamplighter being exceptions. To that list we should add the kilted Scotsman who appeared on signage at EconoLodge, as seen here in 1984.

If the logo for the Prime Way Inn on I-65 in Homewood does not give you the same nostalgic tingle as the other motel signs we have seen, don't feel alone. It just may be the most obscure lodging chain represented in this chapter. But as a bonus, we get to see the building and signage for one of Alabama's few examples of the aforementioned Jerry's Restaurants, presenting a most colorful way to close this chapter.

SIX

KEEP ALABAMA GREEN—
BRING MONEY

In this chapter, we will be taking a brief look at Alabama's tourism industry (brief, because the topic has already been covered in previous books in this series) and other forms of entertainment. From the late 1970s until today, the first sight greeting drivers entering the state from Tennessee on I-65 was this giant missile supplied by Huntsville's Space and Rocket Center. At the time we were going to press, a debate still raged as to whether the decaying relic needed to be scrapped, renovated or re-created in a new form. The countdown continues.

ABOVE: The end of Alabama opposite the I-65 welcome center was the Gulf beaches. This impressive billboard welcomed tourists to Dauphin Island in the 1960s. Like all of Alabama's coastline, Dauphin Island has been wiped clean and rebuilt after numerous hurricanes over the decades, so this masterpiece is necessarily long gone.

OPPOSITE, TOP: In the northwestern quadrant of the state, Dismals Gardens has been an attraction siphoning drivers off US 78 en route between Tupelo and Birmingham. This is how its entrance appeared in the early 1970s; the acreage was alternatively known as Dismals Wonder Gardens.

OPPOSITE, BOTTOM: Noccalula Falls Park has long been a beloved project of the city of Gadsden. This oversized postcard from the late 1960s illustrates some of the various types of signage in the park, from that for the historical Pioneer Museum to the more circus-like Kiddie Korner. It certainly looks like they had kornered plenty of kiddies on the day that photo was taken.

OPPOSITE: Although Rock City was not an Alabama attraction, there was enough traffic passing through on its way to Chattanooga to justify a number of the famous barns in the state. The red one with the shiny black-and-white sign was located near Collinsville in 1992, while the crumbling, rusting example can still be seen (at least for now) on US 11 near Valley Head. Rock City has recently embarked on a project to repaint as many of the existing barn signs as possible. But, as might be expected, such work depends on the cooperation of the property owners.

ABOVE: Southbound drivers on US 11 saw this sign on the opposite side of the "35 Miles" Rock City barn. Beginning in the 1960s, Sequoyah Caverns was operated by longtime Rock City barn painter Clark Byers, so he certainly knew his way around a bucket and brush. Barely visible on the partly collapsed wall is his slogan "World's 9th Wonder." Since the mid-1930s, Byers had painted barn ads promoting Rock City as "World's 8th Wonder," so he was not about to bite the rocky hands that had been feeding him.

ABOVE: Elsewhere along US 11, Clark Byers found this pair of adjacent barns and extended his Sequoyah Caverns advertising onto both of them. The large barn carried the main message, while the smaller shed-type structure continued the ballyhoo by listing "Waterfalls / Lakes." Neither barn exists today.

OPPOSITE: Sequoyah Caverns no doubt still exist but were closed as a tourist attraction in 2013. Four years later, historian Russell Wells documented these remaining signs clustered near the former entrance. Today, a drive along I-59 will show no evidence of Sequoyah Caverns at all, and it takes a sharp eye to find any remnants on US 11 as well. *Both, Russell Wells collection.*

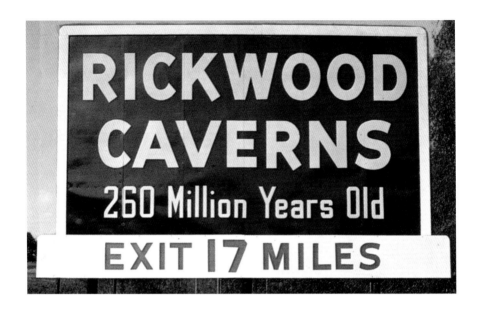

OPPOSITE, TOP: Rickwood Caverns, near Warrior, had been a commercial operation for many years before joining the ranks of Alabama State Parks in 1974. Prior to that, Rickwood's red-and-white billboards could be seen on main highways and back roads alike. This example on I-65 appears to have been one of those but repainted brown to fit with traditional state park signage.

OPPOSITE, BOTTOM: From the 1950s through the 1980s, no road trip was complete without a stop at Stuckey's. Alabama had several of them—except, oddly, none on the entire stretch of I-59. This one was built at the future junction of US 31 and I-65 near Lacon and was almost out of business by the time this photo was taken. The whole Stuckey's chain faced an uncertain future but has recently bounced back, making its candies available along the highways once again.

ABOVE: Stuckey's was known for its hundreds of billboards as much as for its candy and gift shops. This crumbling example could still be seen on US 31 near Morris in 2016. Visible only at certain times of the year, when the foliage was sparse, it has since deteriorated even further and is no longer legible.

ABOVE: Alabama's homegrown answer to Stuckey's was the Saxon's chain, featuring the same combination of candy, souvenirs and snack bars. This was the Saxon's headquarters building on US 431 in Wellington, where the candy was manufactured and packaged by hand. After the death of Henry Saxon in a 1968 automobile accident, his wife, Cora, let the leases on their retail locations expire one by one but continued to sell their candy in other stores for several more years.

OPPOSITE: Yes, there was a time when cellphones did not exist, so travelers who needed to make a call had to rely on pay phones. In 1991, this sign near Jasper announcing such availability was slowly being devoured by the tree on which it had been mounted. Today, the tree and sign have long since hung up and quit.

OPPOSITE, TOP: Atop Red Mountain overlooking downtown Birmingham, "The Club" was unique in incorporating quotation marks into its neon sign. It also appears that someone used the same shade of green paint on the building to paint the grass on the lawn.

OPPOSITE, BOTTOM: Decatur's Funland Park is something of a throwback, with its statue-laden miniature golf course, skating rink and arcade. Even this sign seems somehow reminiscent of an earlier, less technological era.

ABOVE: This one gets the prize for the strangest photo in the book. Way back in the opening pages, we saw yours truly as a puppeteer at Western Hills Mall in 1982. Two years later, I had my first TV series using the same cast of characters, taped on location at various spots around town. One of those was the venerable Kiddieland Park at the Alabama State Fairgrounds, and this is a freeze-frame from the unedited raw footage. One of the original 1947 signs was still there, rusty and with broken neon tubes dangling. Not long after this, the park underwent a renovation that eliminated all such historical artifacts.

ABOVE: Also well-remembered at the fairgrounds was this entrance to the grandstand (also the Birmingham International Raceway), with a neon star and its radiating multicolored beams. Considering that Dixie Neon had recently manufactured the sign for the first Holiday Inn in Alabama, it is not much of a stretch to assume they might have repurposed some of the blueprints for this masterpiece. *Dixie Neon collection.*

OPPOSITE: Bowling was especially popular in the 1950s and early 1960s, and both of these signs date from that period. The Pine Bowl was on US 31 at Fultondale. The forty-eight-lane bowling alley at Eastwood Mall was photographed just before its demolition (along with the rest of the mall) in 2005. The "color bars" on the wall were simply one of those 1960s decor elements that cannot be explained. You had to be there.

OPPOSITE, TOP: Miniature golf was another pastime that saw a rebirth in the post–World War II baby boom era. The former site of Lou's Miniature Golf in Birmingham's East Lake neighborhood is now an exit ramp off I-59. Its neon sign with an animated golf ball must have been something to see at night. *Ace Neon collection.*

OPPOSITE, BOTTOM: Long after a small course in Springville closed, this signboard with the property rules was still hanging on. The impressive artwork brings one question to mind: Who knew miniature golf was so effective for leg muscle development? Apparently, it doesn't work as well for spelling. See how many typos you can find in this piece.

ABOVE: The national chain of Putt-Putt Golf courses had several locations in Alabama, but this photo is notable for showing the original-style neon sign with its animated putter. It is obvious that orange and white was the preferred Putt-Putt color scheme. *Jim Hatcher collection.*

ABOVE: Well, down in Gulf Shores, Zooland Mini-Golf seems to have used all the colors that Putt-Putt Golf turned down. A truly psychedelic example of the game, the course has since changed its name to Tiki Golf but has retained its surrealistic combination of statues and colors.

OPPOSITE: If we had the space—which we don't—we could have filled a chapter with images of movie theaters, both the indoor and outdoor types. We will have to let this single John Margolies image stand in for all of them. He found the crumbling ruin in Selma in 1982, by which time there was no longer any evidence of what name it might have once carried. *John Margolies collection.*

OPPOSITE, TOP: When movie theaters began closing, it was largely due to television. For a number of years, the WAPI call letters were shared by a Birmingham radio station and TV station (Channel 13), and they both operated out of this building with its huge neon sign.

OPPOSITE, BOTTOM: In the early 1960s, Birmingham's WBRC-TV (Channel 6) had two popular afternoon kids' programs: a Bozo the Clown franchise and Benny Carle hosting the Bugs Bunny cartoons. The parking lot for those shows' guests was decorated with this sign, using both Bugs and Bozo to welcome them.

ABOVE: WBRC had a set of enormous red neon letters (still in existence and now the station's logo) facing the downtown side of Red Mountain. However, almost forgotten is that a duplicate set of letters was on the opposite side of the mountain, facing Homewood. This early 1970s view taken during a Fourth of July celebration is one of the only shots showing the "south side" WBRC logo. (Also note the guest parking sign without Bozo and Bugs, as those shows had long since left the air.)

OPPOSITE, TOP: Channel 13's longtime kids' TV star was Cousin Cliff Holman, and in the mid-1950s—while the station was still known as WABT rather than WAPI—an antique car was turned into a sort of "traveling sign" advertising both the station and the star. A loud-yellow vehicle covered in slogans could hardly be ignored as Holman drove it around town to various special events.

OPPOSITE, BOTTOM: For his part, Benny Carle left WBRC and Birmingham in 1964 and moved to the Huntsville TV market. There, his show was outfitted with this space-age set and a sign that dwarfed the host and his diminutive guests. Note all of Carle's sponsors represented on the table behind him, including an early version of Ronald McDonald.

ABOVE: During her travels, photographer Debra Jane Seltzer found these two TV station signs on the outskirts of Dothan. The WDHN sign comes from the early days of color television (note the ABC Network logo), while the WTVY sign marked the former location of that station's studios and tower. *Debra Jane Seltzer collection.*

OPPOSITE: Schools do not exactly fall into the same category as tourism or entertainment, but a few of them deserve to be included somewhere. The Birmingham City Schools venues built during the 1920s generally followed this style of architecture and signage. This 1959 photo of the John J. Eagan School near the American Cast Iron Pipe Company (ACIPCO) was taken for a back-to-school promotion by the downtown Sears store.

ABOVE: In a rather unusual move, when the old Clanton High School was razed, not all of it faced the bulldozer. This, the school's entrance and sign, were left in place as a memorial of sorts. Vintage photos show that this entrance was actually on a corner of the main building.

ABOVE: And speaking of corners, Corner High School in Jefferson County was this author's alma mater. Like so many others, its original 1920s building was eventually demolished to make way for a vacant lot, but this view of the original front entrance was preserved in 2011.

OPPOSITE: The University of Alabama at Birmingham (UAB) began in the 1960s as an offshoot of the main campus in Tuscaloosa. This incredibly simple sign dates from its early days, when its now world-renowned medical center was just getting started. (Note that it was originally named IN Birmingham; it was changed to AT Birmingham some thirty years later.)

UNIVERSITY
OF
ALABAMA
IN
BIRMINGHAM

COLLEGE OF GENERAL STUDIES
MEDICAL COLLEGE
SCHOOL OF DENTISTRY
SCHOOL OF NURSING
SCHOOL OF HEALTH SERVICES
ADMINISTRATION

UNIVERSITY OF ALABAMA
HOSPITALS & CLINICS

In 1965, Berry High School in Vestavia Hills commissioned this amazing mosaic on one of its buildings. At first glance, it appears to be a basketball game, but closer inspection shows that the figures represent different branches of study (arts, humanities, sciences, mathematics and athletics). Even after the campus was renovated into Louis Pizitz Middle School in 2018, the mosaic was preserved as an important artifact. And yes, that school is one of several in the area named after the founder of the Pizitz department stores that we mentioned in the first chapter.

Like schools, churches should serve a more important purpose than entertainment, but since we began this book with a church sign, we might as well bookend it with another one. This open-air tabernacle with its lighted cross was visible on the Bessemer Super Highway until a more modern metal building replaced it in the early 1970s. By now, you should be convinced that signs have served all sorts of purposes in Alabama, from the ridiculous to the sublime, as it were.

BIBLIOGRAPHY

Hollis, Tim. *Birmingham's Theater and Retail District*. Mt. Pleasant, SC: Arcadia Publishing, 2005.

———. *Dixie Before Disney: 100 Years of Roadside Fun*. Jackson: University Press of Mississippi, 1999.

———. *Lost Attractions of Alabama*. Charleston, SC: The History Press, 2019.

———. *See Alabama First*. Charleston, SC: The History Press, 2013.

———. *Vintage Birmingham Signs*. Mt. Pleasant, SC: Arcadia Publishing, 2008.

Jakle, John A., Keith A. Sculle and Jefferson S. Rogers. *The Motel in America*. Baltimore, MD: Johns Hopkins University Press, 1996.

Kazek, Kelly. "Bama's Lost Landmarks." *Birmingham News*, August 20, 2015.

———. "The Story behind Alabama's Other Iron Man Statue." *Birmingham News*, March 12, 2020.

Langdon, Philip. *Orange Roofs, Golden Arches: The Architecture of America's Chain Restaurants*. New York: Alfred A. Knopf, 1986.

Margolies, John, and Emily Gwathney. *Signs of Our Time*. New York: Abbeville Press, 1993.

Sanford, Peggy. "Old McDonald's: Burger Joints of a Bygone Era." *Birmingham News*, November 25, 1984.

ABOUT THE AUTHOR

Tim Hollis has written thirty-eight other books on pop culture history, a number of them concerning southeastern tourism. He also operates his own museum of vintage toys, souvenirs and other pop culture artifacts near Birmingham, Alabama.